Kismet: Destiny,
Three Years Teaching in Turkey

Year One: 2007-2008
Photographs and stories

By
Natalie Plowman

Dedicated to my mother, Charlene, and my father, Bobby. Without your support, through school and life, I never would have had these three years. Thank you for supporting my wanderlust.

**

My obsession with travel could easily have started at a young age, when my dad took me out to a local airport, and stuck me under jets that were taking off just above my head. Maybe I'm confabulating, but I swear I can remember the roaring, deafening sounds screaming overhead, as the planes took off to wherever their destinations might have been.

Or perhaps my obsession with travel was ignited by the heavy amounts of reading I did as a child. Anne Shirley and Laura Ingalls Wilder were both teachers who had a sense of adventure, and they were my childhood heroines. I truly did always have my nose stuck in a book. I would walk from the school bus to my classroom reading a book. My eye doctor told me that I had damaged my eyes from reading next to a tiny nightlight after I was supposed to be asleep, reading for hours in the dark (whether that's actually the cause of my near-sightedness is open to debate). It could have been the excitement of reading about unknown, unexplored places that sowed what would become a monstrous contraption of a seed, rooted deeply inside of me.

Either way, my desire to travel and to experience the unknown has completely consumed my life.

**

2007-2008: The First Year

What exactly possessed me to actively pursue teaching English overseas still mystifies me. The idea came from my favorite high school English teacher and newspaper advisor. When I was 16, she told us about where she had lived and taught overseas, and her stories intrigued me. They intrigued me enough that I majored in English, with a concentration in education. I wanted to teach English, but first, I wanted to do it overseas.

Halfway through my senior year of college, I found myself in Iowa, at an overseas job fair, in the middle of her lung-shattering, icy-cold winter in February: 21, single, and only a student teacher. I had no experience with my own classroom to boast of.

I received loads of inquiring looks, a heavy amount of judgment, and a fair bit of skepticism about my desires and my abilities. I arrived at this recruiting fair, and out of the hundreds of experienced teachers who had been teaching domestically or internationally for years, I was one of the youngest, if not *the* youngest of the crowd. I had never compiled a professional resume before this fair, nor had I ever had a formal job interview for a salaried position. I wound up having three interviews in one day, more scheduled for the following day, and I distributed at least 40 resumes.

At the end of the weekend, after a frazzling experience with a sketchy job offer (and being blatantly put down because of my sex and marital status—"You have to buy a car if you come here, because we don't want to worry about you being depressed and alone in your house on the weekends."), I, by some miracle, stumbled upon a job. My first job in my field of study. Not only was this my first job in the direction of my career-path, but it was also a job teaching English: in Turkey.

The school itself sounds like paradise. It's on cliffs overlooking the Sea of Marmara, the school is for gifted and talented students, and I'll be living in Europe/Asia/the Middle East. I mean really, what more could someone who loves travel, photography, and writing ask for?

I am about to uproot my life and move to where Europe and Asia collide. By myself. Without any clue, really, of what I am doing.

**

Sweltering heat. Delirious, hazy hotness. Cigarette smoke. A headache. A queasy stomach. Thoughts of *"What the hell have I done?"* weaving in and out of my half-functioning mind.

With seven suitcases, and with no idea who was going to be picking me up at the airport ("It'll be taken care of! Don't worry about it!"), I walked through the Istanbul airport's gates into the passenger arrival area, swamped—flooded, with people.

Among the crowd of many, a young man was holding a sign with my name. *Thank goodness.*

Sweating profusely and feeling nauseous (something I ate on the plane? nerves?), I watched, as if removed from reality, as the boy helped me with my bags and took me to a white van waiting outside for me. The driver didn't even acknowledge me; he just shoveled my bags into the back of the van. Then we were on our way. There was no air conditioning in the van, and the sound of air whooshing through the windows is the only sound I remember.

Looking around, exhausted, I gazed at the landscape in horror. Buildings upon buildings upon buildings greeted me. Salmon pinks, leftover blues, and mustard yellows. Mosques popped up everywhere along the landscape. Where was I? Being so accustomed to the open landscape of Colorado's plains and mountains, I was completely unprepared for what a city of 20 million people would look like, smell like, feel like. The claustrophobia of the city confounded and overwhelmed me.

As we crossed one of the two bridges to get to the Asian side of Turkey, I looked below me at the massive Bosphorus, happy for a tinge of beauty. But even the ships on the straight felt foreign to me. Overwhelmed, I closed my eyes and slept. I slept until we reached the school, as if by shutting my eyes I could close out the reality of where I was and what I had done.

**

I was greeted with a cup of water at the guard shack of the school's entrance. I could only take a couple of sips of the warm water out of politeness, because my stomach had already knotted itself with anxiety.

The driver and the student who picked me up from the airport quickly ushered me to my apartment. It all seemed to happen faster than I could register. They unloaded the seven bags, repeatedly walked up and down the multiple flights of stairs, dropped them in the entryway to my apartment, and left. No instructions, no tour of where I was welcomed me to my new home. And then, there I was: alone in an empty apartment.

I walked into the bedroom after moving my luggage inside to the living room, sat down on the bed, and wept.

What was I thinking? I left behind my perfectly happy life to live in the middle of nowhere, in a country I know nothing about. My family, my friends, my boyfriend, my home, my mountains...everything is gone. All of my comforts. Why had I thought that this would be a good idea? I am all alone.

I made my bed, and went to sleep, exhausted and depressed, leaving everything else packed up and untouched in the suitcases.

**

I woke up the next morning and went to breakfast at the dining hall. My stomach felt tight and queasy, and I was still in a state of shock. Breakfast consisted of cheeses, tomatoes, cucumbers, olives, bread with various spreads, and tea. None of this appealed to me. I wanted comfort, I wanted familiarity (sugary cereal, please?), and nothing about this was comfortable. I ate breakfast with an elderly couple at the school for a conference, and even though they spoke to me in English, I hardly understood a word of what they said. I picked at my breakfast, and my stomach continued to tie itself into knots, as I became less and less comfortable.

I went home and slept again. I awoke with an upset stomach, and went back to sleep. This cycle repeated itself for two days. Upset stomach, sleep, upset stomach, sleep. I ate and drank less and less. I lay in bed for two days, without leaving my apartment. I had no idea how to use my phone, no access to the internet, and no t.v. I only laid in bed, with the early morning call to prayer occasionally waking me up around 5:30 a.m.

Two co-workers, with whom I'd only met briefly, started bringing me fruit and water, since I felt too ill to even walk up to the dining hall. It was as if my body and mind had resolved to give up and shut down, overwhelmed by the transition. Soon, I couldn't even drink the water they'd brought me without getting sick to my stomach. Nothing would stay down. So I went back to bed, and slept again.

I had restless dreams, and the heat was unbearable. I didn't have a fan or air conditioning in my apartment. I felt delusional. My mind was stuck on repeat: *I can't stay here. I have to go back home. I shouldn't have left. This was a huge, huge mistake. I have to go home. I'll have my dad pay for the ticket, and I'll somehow reimburse him. I have to leave.*

I didn't unpack my bags for four days, because I was convinced that I was going to leave.

With these thoughts stewing in my head, I stayed in bed, and grew weaker.

**

One morning, a co-worker knocked on my door to bring me food, and I couldn't even stand up straight because I was so weak. As she looked at me, cowering in my doorway, she decided that I needed to go to the nurse (being a boarding school, there was one conveniently located on campus). She sent down a man to my apartment who, if I believed in angels, was definitely my guardian angel.

His name was Serkan. He spoke perfect English, and patiently escorted me up the 100+ steps to get to the nurse's office. The nurse was concerned after listening to my racing heart, so sent me to the hospital. My heart was only racing because of the intense heat and the walk up all of the stairs, but I didn't argue with her. I felt too weak to protest. I wanted someone to fix me.

**

Next, I was in a van that was taking me to a nearby hospital. My principal (this was the first time I'd met him) accompanied me, along with my Turkish guardian angel. Waiting at the hospital, I looked around in shock. Again, with the heat pressing down on my shoulders, I felt anxious. All around me were women wearing headscarves, men smoking (yes, in the hospital), and the potent odor of b.o., which contributed to my nausea. Everything was unfamiliar.

7

The first doctor who looked at me asked questions via my translator/protector, until I realized that I needed to puke again. So I did, and she sent me to get blood work done. I felt mortified that this man was watching me puke and asking me questions like: did I have diarrhea? How often? But my mortification gradually faded, as I felt increasingly worse. I just wanted someone to take care of me. (Side note: there isn't a personal 'bubble' in Turkey, like there is in the U.S. This was when the walls of my bubble started to thin a little, as I realized I needed others to look after me for a little while.)

After taking a urine sample, that I then had to walk across the hospital to give back to the nurses (hey everyone! Look at what I'm holding!), I was taken into another room, where I had to lie down and wait. My guardian tried to make small talk and joke around with me, to make me feel better. I can't even imagine what he was thinking about this pitiful mess of a female in front of him, but he was only kind. I was so weak, and my brain was still so overwhelmed from my transition, that I could hardly respond to his conversation. I was terrified, being in a hospital in a strange, foreign city, where people were smoking inside. There seemed to be a general lack of organization and only utter chaos—not what anyone wants to see in a hospital, especially when the language is an unfamiliar one.

A woman came in with a needle in her hand (because who doesn't want an injection in a foreign hospital?) and told me in Turkish (and then gestured to me) to turn over onto my stomach. *Oh dear god. Do people really still give injections this way?*

Yes, and I was so lucky that I got two. One in each cheek. And no, I'm not talking about the sometimes rosy-colored cheeks on my face. I didn't even know what I was being injected with. I just trusted that the power of medicine would heal me, even if I was in a country that was new to me.

I had an IV inserted into my arm, which also horrified me, as I'd never had an IV before. I don't have a great track record with needles; I've been known to grow dizzy, and, even on occasion, faint. When the IV was inserted, I immediately began puking into a bedpan that was handed to me, which smelled of ancient urine. Apparently I was puking on my hair (I really wasn't paying attention at this point), because my guardian went to get tissues and proceeded to pull my hair back, as I emptied my stomach of whatever could possibly be left in there.

I had to lie there for about 45 minutes while I was re-hydrated by the IV. My protector stayed by my side the entire time, and told me I was starting to regain color in my face. I remember thinking: how could a complete stranger have such immense kindness to take care of me? I was vomiting all over myself, and a urine-encrusted bedpan, and still, he sat there and made encouraging remarks. He even gave me his mp3 player to listen to, and I was comforted as the Counting Crows started to play. It was something familiar.

I started to feel better, as I sensed life seeping, dribbling back into my body.

**

I came 'home' to my apartment, still culture-shocked, but feeling a little better after having met one of the most hospitable people I've ever known, and better after having my body pumped full of hydrating fluids. I couldn't believe that this man, who I'd only met that morning, had taken me to the hospital, translated for me the entire time, and stayed by my side all day. He did so for absolutely nothing in exchange, and with a sunny disposition the entire time. My principal had paid for my hospital bills, even though I wasn't technically working at the school yet. All of this kindness really struck me, and I started to understand that I couldn't really leave this place. Not yet. Maybe no one had shown me around or taken care of me for the first few days, but I was certainly being cared for now. I made a compromise with myself that I needed to stay at least one year of my two-year contract. I needed to give it a chance.

Oh, and the blood tests at the hospital revealed some sort of bacteria in my system (food poisoning, or something perhaps from the airplane). I took some strange pills for a few days, as instructed by the doctors at the hospital. Those, or something else, proceeded to make my teeth ache for several days.

I woke up the morning after my day at the hospital, and the sun was shining directly into my room. I felt much more like myself, and my curiosity kicked in. I left my apartment, and began to explore my school's campus.

The campus is adorned with all sorts of vegetation: beautiful flowers growing in trees and on bushes, olive trees, fig trees, apple trees...there's a lovely Greek temple on the campus which overlooks the Sea of Marmara. The school is perched on cliffs right above the sea.

It really does look like paradise.

Above: The sunrise out of my window the first morning that I felt better. The first morning I realized that I would be okay in Turkey.

Photos of the school:

The Greek temple on campus

The sea and train tracks below the school

The building I lived in

**

When I finally had enough strength to eat food, and enough courage to talk to my new co-workers, I gradually started to feel more comfortable. I hadn't been in contact with anyone from home yet, so went to find a computer that I could e-mail with. My laptop in my apartment had yet to be connected to the internet (only after about two months of living here, did I finally have internet in my apartment).

I found a computer in the administrative office that I used every morning after breakfast to catch up on my e-mails. That was what I looked forward to every day: the time when I could have contact with my family and friends from back home. My e-mails home looked like mini essays.

The secretary in the office didn't speak any English, and I had yet to speak a word of Turkish, but I would always smile at her, and she would smile and nod back at me. I wondered what she thought of me, the weird girl who came into the office to e-mail for almost an hour every day, laughing and tearing up at various electronic letters from home.

One morning, as I was e-mailing, she said "Natalie?" (Everyone in Turkey pronounced my name properly, like 'Nat-a-lee,' not the slurred American pronunciation of 'Nadulee'). I turned my head, and she said "çay (chai)?" Knowing this to be the Turkish word for tea, I nodded eagerly. That morning, as I sat e-mailing, tea was delivered to me by the school's lovely tea lady, just because of the thoughtful secretary. I loved these random moments, because even these tiniest acts of thoughtfulness helped me to heal and move forward from the life I'd left behind. They reminded me of the adventurous spirit that drew me to this unfamiliar country in the first place, and how much excitement I had ahead of me.

**

My first venture out of the school and into Istanbul was with a co-worker, Sarah. She had been to Istanbul before, so had a better sense of direction than I did. Kind of.

We walked up the cobblestone roads in the scorching heat, and she showed me around the Sultanahmet area, the most touristy district of Istanbul. We saw the Blue Mosque one day, and went into the Hagia Sophia the next.

The Hagia Sophia is absolutely extraordinary. I couldn't believe the inside...the intricate and extensive and *massive* beauty of the place is unsurpassed in my eyes. I actually had tears in my eyes, moved by its precise and meticulous splendor, and I was overwhelmed by imagining the immense amount of history contained by the building, and what had yet to be uncovered beneath it.

It was a reminder of how feeble my mind is, that unfortunately, it has no concept or no frame of reference to even begin to grasp how long that structure has been standing. I tried to imagine what that building meant to people when it was a church, and then when it was a mosque. I wondered about what the people were like at the time it was built, and all throughout the time it has been standing. I wonder if humans are exactly the same now as they were then, and if only the situations that we face and our historical contexts are different.

I had goose bumps, imagining what lay beneath the building, what sorts of secrets are woven into the structure, and how much of what lies beneath it is still undiscovered. It was absolutely mind-boggling to ponder these structures, being in a city of such ancient mysteries. These elusive whisperings create a breeze of inexplicably haunting feelings that wind through the city.

Photos from Istanbul:

Above: Inside the Hagia Sophia

The Hagia Sophia

Above: The Blue Mosque

**

Next, I must introduce you to Ed. He was a very large part of my first few months at the school.

One evening, as I was turning off the lights in my living room, and about to go to sleep, I noticed something in the corner of my apartment. I walked over to take a closer look, and there, legs poking out from his hole in the wall, was the biggest spider I had ever seen. It was at least the biggest spider that I'd ever seen inside a house.

Allow me to mention the fact that I am not at all fond of spiders. After a black widow incident as a child, and a few wolf spider encounters in one of my college apartments, I was pretty much done with any spider bigger than my thumbnail.

I took a few deep breaths after I saw him, and realized that the wall he was poking out of also bordered my bedroom wall. I knew I wouldn't sleep, imagining him crawling back under the other side of the wall and into my bedroom (and then crawling on me at night while I was sleeping). I tiptoed into my room, and took a look at the wall beside by my bed. There were wads of tissue stuffed under the gap in the wall. The previous owner had obviously known about the spider, and had the same thoughts I did.

I was a little comforted knowing that obviously the spider was pretty stationary, if he had been there for so long. But I still attempted to get rid of him. Vacuums, scissors--nothing worked. He was too quick for me. Any time I approached him, he would dart back underneath the wall and into his lair.

Finally, one night, after repeated murder attempts, I sat down next to the wall and spoke to Ed (I had named the spider Ed, to make him a little less terrifying). I actually spoke out loud (one sign that living alone has driven you to a new level of crazy): "Ed. I'll make a deal with you. I'll let you live, as long as you never move from that spot."

And so, Ed became my roommate:

Photos of Istanbul and the Black Sea:

Istanbul (above)

The Bosphorus opening up into the Black Sea.

A ship on the Bosphorus in the pouring rain.

A generous amount of rain

Rainy day near the Black Sea.

**

Teaching. I had experience in the classroom before, and I had student-taught. But nothing really prepares you for having your own classroom. I should also mention that there wasn't really a curriculum for me to follow; I essentially had to design my own. This is just slightly intimidating for a first-year teacher.

My first step was to figure out what to teach, and how. I asked one of my 10th grade classes what kinds of books they liked to read. A few raised their hands and said 'history.' I was trying to think of a history novel that would fit their interests but also their English level. Elie Weisel's *Night* came to mind. I had helped a teacher with the novel a couple of years back, and had read it myself when I was a 9th grader. It seemed like a good fit.

I asked if they had ever read anything on the Holocaust or World War II. Several heads shook no. I asked if they were interested in reading about the Holocaust. A hand raised, and a student asked: "What's the Holocaust?" I felt goose bumps creeping up my arms. I asked if any of them knew what the Holocaust was. Most of them weren't really familiar with it, had heard about it in passing. Perhaps they didn't know the English word for it. Turkey wasn't really involved in World War II, so a lot of issues surrounding the time period aren't really taught, from what I've heard and gathered. Genocide is also a touchy issue, given the Turkish history with the Aremenians.

I proceeded to teach a unit on prejudice, World War II, and stereotypes. I had a student stay after class almost every day and ask me questions for hours: 'How do you know that the Jews didn't control the economy?' and 'Why are Americans so sympathetic toward the Jews?' 'How do you know that Hilter wasn't justified in his plans?'

I actually loved getting the questions, because it made me feel like my lessons were accomplishing something, plus I had to do my own research. Growing up in schools in the U.S., we usually don't ask these questions. We're so horrified by what we've been shown, that there doesn't always seem to be a need to probe deeper into the philosophy behind the events. But, having a student ask me these questions encouraged me to back up my answers as much as I could. Not only was I teaching, I was getting the opportunity to learn things.

**

After a few weeks of adjustment, I decided that it was time to christen my kitchen. I just spent the summer leading up to my departure cooking dinners on an almost nightly basis for my friends, sister, roommate, and boyfriend. Cooking and baking are two hobbies that I truly adore, and that bring me peace.

After buying the ingredients (flour, salt, baking soda, chocolate bars instead of chocolate chips--I hadn't discovered their existence in Turkey yet--, and butter), I found a chocolate chip cookie recipe to bake one night. I rolled up my sleeves, and used whatever kitchen materials I could find in order to bake up a batch of cookies.

I didn't have measuring cups, so I used a coffee mug to measure out my flour and sugar. I didn't have measuring spoons, so I estimated with the baking soda and salt. I cut up the chocolate bar into little chocolate chunks. I mixed everything together in a cooking pot (I was lacking a mixing bowl), and lined my oven shelf with aluminum foil. As the cookies baked in my oven, my house filled with the aroma of warm chocolate. I turned my music up louder, and danced around my apartment while I cleaned up my mess.

My oven's temperature dial is in Celsius, and it only continues to get hotter the longer it's on. It doesn't stay at the temperature where it has been set. If I'm baking three batches of cookies, the first one may need to bake for 11 minutes, the second one for eight minutes, and the third one for five minutes.

Finally, it appeared that the cookies were ready. I took them out of the oven and moved them to a plate. They smelled amazing.

I took a bite into my first chocolate chip cookie baked in Turkey...

And promptly spit it out.

They tasted like pure salt! I knew I had followed the recipe correctly, so what had I done wrong? I searched about for my ingredients, and finally looked at the bag of sugar. It said 'tuz' on it.

Tuz means salt in Turkish. Instead of using a cup of sugar, I had used a cup of salt.

**

Apart from my two 10th grade classes, I was also endowed with two prep-level classes. They were sections created for the students who had little to no English experience. At the start of the year, I had some students who only knew how to say "Hi, how are you?"

Again, I had no idea how I was supposed to teach them. No guidelines, no curriculum. My ESL experience was minimal, but the lack of any material or instruction for how the class was supposed to look left me scrambling before school started. The first few weeks of school were full of me acting things out in front of them, speaking slowly, having students translate what I was saying to the rest of the class, and drawing a lot on the board (my terrible stick figure drawings quickly became a comical topic).

At the same time, I was trying to learn some Turkish. I wanted to know enough to at least be able to get around. Two older students were teaching a group of us foreign teachers Turkish once a week. Our lessons were held in an empty classroom from 9-10 p.m., one of the students' only free hours on campus.

One day, I had a Turkish exam to prepare for. During a five-minute break in my prep class, I was skimming through my flashcards. Some of my prep students were helping me study. One student asked me to write 'boring' on the board (in Turkish). So I wrote: 'sikici.' Immediately, the students' faces became mortified, some were bright red. One girl came up to erase it instantly. "Ms. P, no! That's a bad word! No, that's not it!" I was so confused! I remembered the word I had written on the board being the word for boring!

I asked, "What did I write? What did I say?" They shook their heads. No, it was too bad to say out loud.

I found out later by asking a co-worker, that I had basically written 'fuck' on the board. In Turkish there is an 'i' and an un-dotted i: 'ı'. I should have used the 'ı'. That little difference proved to be a world of difference.

Oops.

**

I quickly became known as the cookie lady. After my first unsuccessful experiment, I began baking on a regular basis. I gave cookies to my co-workers, and to students who stopped by. It was my way of connecting with other people. It was my way of relieving stress (and simply a way of filling empty time). This contributed to the start of my cooking club.

Six students, ranging from ages 13-17, stopped by my apartment for two hours every Sunday night, where I attempted to teach them to cook. Of course, each meeting had to end with baking some kind of dessert (for the first half of the year, it was only chocolate chip cookies). We cooked salmon, pastas, chicken, breakfast for dinner, and homemade pizzas (the all-time favorite—each student made his/her own pizza). For desserts, we experimented with shortbread, brownies, chocolate fondue, and multiple types of cookies. Every Sunday night, my empty apartment was filled with music, the smells of olive oil, garlic, and then baking chocolate. Every Sunday night, I had laughter and life in my home.

**

One evening, after an hour of happily composing numerous letters, and consuming a glass of sub-par Turkish wine, I got up to turn on music that had long since stopped playing, and to close my window...it's getting chilly here at night! As I closed the window, I happened to glance up at the beaming, lemony moon and thought to myself: "Why, I ought to see if I can photograph the moon over the sea!" I went into my room to fetch my camera.

But I stopped before I reached the hallway.

Because there, on the floor, in the middle of the hallway, was a monstrous, leggy spider. Oh dear god. Its massive, hairy brown legs stretched out in front of him as he sat there (yes, I made him a 'he'), content, apparently.

My heart started racing. *Is it Ed? I haven't seen Ed in a while. Did he re-locate? He's facing my bedroom. Ohmygod please don't go into my bedroom. I have to kill him. I must find the capacity deep within myself to kill this thing that terrifies me...*

I ran into my entryway to grab a tennis shoe, and then tiptoed back to Ed (or his twin). *I'm sorry Ed, but you can't say here anymore...our deal was that you stay in that EXACT same spot under the wall...*but I couldn't do it. I couldn't kill the blasted spider. So, I ran next door to Sarah.

I asked her if she could come kill my spider. She obliged. She hit him with one straight shot of a shoe, and the spider was gone. As she left, she said, "I don't know if he was big enough to be Ed..."

But, I never saw Ed again.

**

The Turkish bath house: hamam. An experience all women should have at some point in their lives. There aren't enough words to describe the paradox of a culture that encourages women to cover up, and a hamam which encourages women to uncover all, while they are scrubbed, washed and massaged by older, half-naked, voluptuous Turkish women.

The bathhouse that I found myself in was built in 1584. It was interesting to think (as I was lying completely unclothed on a hot marble table, staring up at the ceiling) how many thousands of women had been there, and what they were going through in their own personal lives, and historically. I was having a *The Red Tent* moment--women being completely comfortable with their bodies, lounging together, bathing each other, comfortable being around each other...it was a really interesting experience.

America is a culture that preaches about identity and individuality, and then makes women feel ashamed or inadequate about their bodies. Sitting on a huge marble table with excessively endowed, jolly Turkish women, I did not feel judged. It felt natural to me, in some strange way. Why are women so uncomfortable being vulnerable around other women? Again, my mind flickered back to *The Red Tent*. Isn't that how it's supposed to be? Women taking care of each other?

**

Istanbul:

The Turkish policeman who are posted around the city, and their weapons

View of the street from the hotel window

**

"Let's consider Emptiness in general for a moment...what is it about fresh snow, clean air, pure water? Or good music? As Claude DeBussy expressed it, 'Music is the space between the notes.'

Like silence after noise, or cool, clear water on a hot, stuffy day, Emptiness cleans out the messy mind and charges up the batteries of spiritual energy.

Many people are afraid of Emptiness, however, because it reminds them of Loneliness...So some of us do instead, and after discarding the emptiness of the Big Congested Mess, we discover the Fullness of Nothing..."

--*The Tao of Pooh*, Benjamin Hoff

Living alone and living in an isolated area provides a lot of time for nothingness. A lot of time for thinking. A lot of time for loneliness. This is something I struggle with frequently. After some time living alone in Turkey, I've come to terms with it, and have learned how to revel in my aloneness. That doesn't mean that it's always easy or enjoyable. But I think it's important to have time alone. It's in those moments alone that you can really understand what's valuable and what's not. It's in those moments that the people who mean the most in your life pull through for you...or don't.

**

October hit, and I was aching for autumn. Turkey doesn't have a clear or pronounced fall, or at least not the area I was living in. Being from Colorado, I missed the exquisite changing of seasons, the beautiful colors that come along with the change, and the feeling of transition that is so necessary for me to feel. I never realized before how important it is for me to actually feel the shifting of the seasons. It signifies a change, it shows that time is indeed, moving forward. In Turkey, I felt as if I was stuck. I never had a very clear adjustment; it just went from being hot to grey and rainy. I longed for a glimpse into autumn. My internal clock felt off without it. One of my dearest friends from Colorado sent me an envelope with a yellow aspen leaf in it, and it brought tears to my eyes.

With a four-day weekend coming up, I decided to go to Munich. I thought I'd at least get an autumn fix there, and I've always wanted to go to Germany. I have a lot of German heritage, and have always felt a pull to visit the place.

With no one else to go with, I decided to go on my own. It was the first time I'd ever traveled alone.

**

I am a cliché, as I'm writing at this café in Munich. I'm at a café in Hofgarten. It's near a park where leaves are falling when slight breezes rustle them, German murmurs are being whispered all around me, and the comforting scent of crisp leaves is wafting around me. And I'm sipping an amazingly delicious, lightly colored beer.

The sun is shining just so through the leaves, and it is chilly...the clock tower is chiming, and I tighten my scarf around my neck.

Old men in long coats walk around puffing on pipes, and the city is filled with bicyclists.

It's strange, but all of the people here seem so elegant and beautiful.

As I let the warmth of the beer peruse my body, I bask in the atmosphere of autumn. October. I feel a sense of urgency, as if I'm pressed for time, but I realize that I am quite at my leisure. I am free to go wherever or do whatever I please. My sense of panic induced by a day of travel subsides...

As I arrived and sat on the train from the airport into Munich, all I could think of as I watched the tumbling greens and autumn crimsons and pumpkin oranges flashing by, was, I belong here. I don't know why. The thought arrived in my mind that this will be a moment that I have been anticipating all of my life.

The beauty here draws tears from my eyes. It is inexplicable.

**

The beer hall experience is something else. I felt a bit timid going into a giant beer hall alone, but you're never alone in a beer hall, I quickly learned. The beer hall I happened to enter into first was filled with smoke and loud chatter. There are large tables everywhere, and you sit wherever there's an open seat. I sat at the far end of a table, a little bit alone. Soon enough, a couple came and sat down by me. They happened to be Americans, and were fascinated to hear about what I was doing in Turkey. They were a little loud, and I noticed that people began to move away from us. I shrunk down in my booth, thinking: *this is why people don't like Americans...this is where we get the bad reputation...*

The couple ended up buying my drink though, so I can't really say anything too bad about them. It was nice to have the company, embarrassing or not.

I strolled around, bought some sugared almonds, listened to street musicians playing melodic classical music.

I went to another beer hall, Hofbrauhaus, where some of the Nazi party meetings were held. I sat at a table with a Bavarian yodeler who had just had an album released that day, and was buying pretzels and beers left and right.

There are yodeling albums?

I quickly became a part of the fuzzy, blurring, loud, smoky atmosphere, and felt myself a part of the environment. There is such a sense of joviality and kinship. A woman walked around selling pretzels, music was blaring...everyone seemed to be content and friendly.

**

I decided to take a train south to Garmisch-Partenkirchen to see if I could go to the famed Neuschwanstein castle. The train ride alone was breath-taking. All of a sudden, the magnificent Bavarian Alps are tumbling in on the horizon. I have never seen mountains like them. I truly felt like I was entering into a fairytale.

I stepped out of the train, and walked into a WC (water closet), where I tiredly stumbled into the men's bathroom, and proceeded to walk in on a man utilizing the facilities.

Yes, I can navigate Munich's subway system late at night, but I can't navigate restrooms in broad daylight. Instead of turning around and leaving, I ran into a stall and hid until everyone was gone, entirely mortified.

I started to feel a little disoriented, and started to become a bit anxiety-ridden. I didn't know where to go or what to do next. I knew absolutely nothing of the town. I had been planning on going directly to the castle (the tour book made it seem like it was closer than it was), but I missed the last bus to the castle for the day. I had to wait until the next morning.

The woman I asked about the bus ticket then proceeded to tell me that there was probably not going to be a train back to Munich the following day, because of a strike that was going on. I started to feel even more panicky, thinking that I was stranded in the south of Germany.

I was overwhelmed by isolation that afternoon. I was anxious and exhausted and was wondering what I'd been thinking, traveling alone. It's un-grounding, uncomfortable, and stressful. I had to make all of my own decisions, and no one was there to help decide, no one to share my thoughts with. There was not even a common language to communicate in.

After panicking for a while, I told myself to calm down. It's okay to feel lonely. Instead of worrying about it, I should just accept it and learn how to deal with it. After I bought some cards and sat in the sun writing letters for a while, I felt a great deal better.

**

I can now easily believe in fairies, goblins and witches after traversing through the forests of Germany. I can readily believe they exist here in this bewitching region. I glance back at the Neuschwanstein castle; it is blanketed in clouds, and I can no longer make out its form.

I had the strangest experience here. I walked to the town near the castle, and was enchanted by the damp, crisp air, the miles of green, and the absolute peaceful calm. Walking back to the castle, I felt an oppressive loneliness, and all of a sudden, I felt like I no longer knew who I was. I was in such a remote, foreign place, that all of my past, my home, and my relationships seemed as if they were from another life. I felt that my identity was no longer attached to me. I really think that this place bewitched me; it was as if I was under a spell. No one knew where I was at this exact moment.

I saw myself as an ant, the speck of life that I actually am in this world, this world of life that is so intricate and complex and so beyond our comprehension. How dare we try to explain it away with religion and science, when they are not even remotely adequate enough? I realized that who I was at that moment, didn't even really matter: I was invisible. No one saw me but myself at that moment, and I had lost myself.

**

I was overwhelmed by the beauty and excessive charm of this place. If only I could accurately paint an image of this area with my mediocre words. Maybe it's the air, the pure, sweet air...the ivory-white and chocolate brown cottages that dot the landscape, the multi-colored flowers spilling from every nook and cranny. Maybe it's because it's autumn, and the trees are of rusty brown, red and orange attire. The surplus of wood piles and the smoke streaming from chimneys, the hawks circling over the pastures frequented by cows with bells around their thick, stocky necks, the men and women wrapped in scarves and hats who are biking around the villages. The desperately quiet forest paths strewn with fallen leaves...all of these ingredients combined cook up enchantment.

**

By my last morning in Munich, I was ready to be done traveling alone. I was sitting in the subway station, on my way back to the airport, when I almost (or did) started having an anxiety attack. My heart started racing, and I felt weighed down by my isolation. It's a strange feeling, traveling alone. No one knows where you are; no one really cares. It is almost an out of body experience. But I remember that trip so vividly and in such great detail, because of the fact that I was alone. I had no one to bounce thoughts or reactions off of, so I recorded them in depth in my journal, and in my memory. Looking back, I feel like I remember every single minuscule detail. And I love that trip.

Photos from Munich:

Neuschwanstein Castle

Biking in Munich

Beer garden in Munich

Fall colors I missed so much

**

After my trip to Munich, I started to feel more comfortable being on my own and traveling alone. I started to enjoy the anonymity of being in a crowded city like Istanbul. I think that the experience is accentuated by being in a foreign country, where you don't speak the language.

Journal entry:

I am invisible to the world right now. I have no duties, no obligations, and no worries. I am invisible. No one knows or cares where I am, or what I'm doing, or who I'm with. No one is expecting me; no one takes notice of me. I am invisible. I am just another head bobbing up and down in a crowd of bustling people. I am just another customer. Just another writer. I am just another woman, reading in a coffee shop. I am invisible. There is no one to hold me accountable. There is no one to remind me of my identity or who I am.

There is no one to sit next to me as I read. There is no one to laugh to about the experiences of the afternoon. All of my thoughts and dialogues are internalized. The hums and echoes of the reverberating voices are not being contributed to by my voice. I am unheard.

There is no one to help me travel or find my way, no one to hold me accountable or to check up on me.

No one is expecting me to feel or react or behave in a certain way, or view things in a certain light.

I am invisible.

**

After a thought-provoking, anxiety-ridden, solo journey, my family arrived in Istanbul for a week of traveling with me, with only joy and anticipation on my side. After a day in Istanbul, we flew to Izmir and traveled to Selçuk to see Mary's house, the Basilica of St. John, and Ephesus. We also visited the Temple of

Artemis (or what's left of it), which was one of the seven wonders of the ancient world.

Visiting ancient ruins like this is always a mixed experience for me. I love history, and I love seeing the ancient sites, but it also brings up frustrations. It's just interesting to think how most everything from that time period is so fuzzy and suspect, but people believe blindly in everything they're told. The fact that Mary's house was found based off a vision of a nun's set me off on a rollercoaster of thought, wondering how much of what we know about history is actually true.

**

The place that is probably dearest to my heart in Turkey is Şirence. My family and I visited the little Greek village early one morning. The stone streets are lined with women selling herbs, teas, olive oil soaps, hand made laces, sweaters and cloths. There are an abundance of wine shops selling local wines and olive oils.

It was quiet and peaceful. The smell of smoke drifting from chimneys created a comfortable atmosphere. We walked around, exploring the cobblestone streets. I saw a woman cooking outside on the patio of her home: green peppers sizzling in a pan, using a jug of olive oil from those very hills. The beautiful green hills were adorned with olive trees and fruit trees.

We stopped at the most quaint and charming café owned by a German man, where we all had (arguably) the best coffee we remembered having, at least in a very long time. Each mug of coffee was adorned with a homemade cinnamon sugar cookie. My sister and I also ordered fresh clotted cream with mulberry sauce that the German man had prepared himself, right there in that café.

We sat lethargically in the sun, basking in a coffee-fied stupor. We ambled down the hill, and headed off to Kuşadası to see the Aegean Sea. But that morning in Şirence with my family is still one of my favorite moments in Turkey. And when I later returned to the city with a different crowd, it was not nearly the same.

**

Photos from the week with my family:

The following photos are from the little Greek village of Şirence:

My sister, walking up the steps.

The following photos are from the ruins at Ephesus:

**

Before I came to Turkey, I used to love to work out at my university's rec center. How spoiled I was. At least 20 elliptical machines, 25 treadmills, a weight room, an indoor track, a swimming pool, T.V.'s...At my school here in Turkey, there is a gym with a few weights and a broken bike. The bike still pedals, it just doesn't function electronically.

Today, as I walked to the gym, anxious to work away my fuzzy state of mind caused by the drizzly weather, I looked out to the sea. The illusion created by the weather and the sunlight made it look like the sun was in the sea. It wasn't, obviously, it was hidden behind clouds, but on the sea, the sun's reflection was beaming its full figure across the water, and its golden rays were leaking into the skies. I thought it...beautiful, that I could see the sun in the sea, but not in the sky.

I went to ride on the broken bike, but this time, encountered about five male students who were also in the room (usually I'm alone, and prefer working out alone). I decided to continue to workout, despite being a bit uncomfortable being in front of students. I was very eager to burn away some stress. I started to pedal away on the broken bike, only to be approached by a boy two minutes later. I pulled out an earphone.

"Yes?"

"Miss P, can I take your shoes please?"

"Um...what the...why do you need to take my shoes?" [Insert note here: Turkey is a culture very big on the removal of shoes before entering a house, however, I had yet to hear anything about the lack of shoes in a gym, for obvious safety reasons].

I was then told that we needed to work out without our shoes, because they were dirty, and the floor needed to remain clean. All sorts of inappropriate expletives ran through my head. How were students expected to work out and lift weights without shoes on? I turned around to look, and sure enough, these boys were lifting without shoes.

I grumbled and removed my shoes and continued pedaling, shoeless.

...Only to be interrupted by another one of my students a few minutes later, asking me if I was crying.

"Um no, that's sweat. Yes, I sweat when I work out, but thanks for the concern." (So unlady-like!)

He continued to ask if I'd like him to open a window or a door. They did seem genuinely concerned about my well-being [insert another note: cardio exercises like running and biking aren't as big in Turkey as they are in America, and I don't recall seeing women partaking in these cardio exercises very much either].

Despite their honest efforts to make me comfortable, it for some reason made me even more grumbly and cranky.

At this point, I'm thinking how I loathe living where I work. I can't even work out in peace. But only for a split second did this cross my mind. Then I started feeling sorry for these poor male students, who were probably bewildered by their odd American English teacher and her strange ways.

Why is she riding the broken bike? Why does she exercise with her shoes on? Why is she sweating/crying? As if in answer to my thoughts about these cultural differences, the call to prayer belted out in the distance from the nearby village.

The students left, and I found myself alone again.

Even if it sometimes appears backwards here to me, even if it sometimes appears that the sun is glimmering in the sea instead of in the sky, I can't help but laugh to myself, and love where I'm living.

**

Winter here is depressing. I never realized how much I needed Colorado's constant sunshine. I never realized how much the weather actually does affect my mood.

I downloaded Skype onto my computer (where you can talk to and see the person you're chatting with). One afternoon, I came home and saw that my dad was calling me on Skype. I answered, and saw my uncle in the background, as well as my half-brother-in-law.

When I saw them in the webcam, I started tearing up, and when I got off the phone, I just started bawling. Seeing my family together, and listening to my mom tell me how it was the first snowfall in Colorado, made me want to be home. The next day was Thanksgiving, and it was the first time I'd been away from my family for a holiday.

The dismal feeling of winter is accented by the long weekend out in the middle of nowhere. With nowhere to go and nothing to do, the grey clouds seem all the more oppressive.

**

Ortaköy is probably my favorite spot in Istanbul. It's located right next to the Bosphorus, and right next to the first bridge (the one that lights up at night with various colors). On Saturdays and Sundays, there is a huge bazaar that lines the cobblestone streets. There are women and men selling pashminas, scarves, earrings, necklaces, magnets, prints, and every other little trinket imaginable. Most of my jewelry has been purchased here.

Fishermen line the area next to the Bosphorus, and pigeons cluster together in the center area, between the water and the restaurants. There are stalls selling kumpir (baked potatoes), waffles (you can choose toppings to put on a freshly-baked waffle: fruits, chocolate sauce, pistachios), and gözleme stands. Gözleme is perhaps one of my favorite Turkish foods, in all of its simplicity. A light tortilla-like dough is stuffed with potatoes, cheese and spinach, and baked like a quesadilla of sorts. You can buy a waffle or kumpir, and walk along the water's edge, watching the fishermen or the tourists walking by.

Occasionally the mosque's call to prayer will ring out. At night, it's great to eat at one of the restaurants with a view of the bridge, watching the green, blue, and purple lights rotating over the Bosphorus.

Fisherman in Ortaköy

Mosque in Ortaköy

Along the streets of Ortaköy

Gazing at the Bosphorus, maybe wanting a bite to eat!

Ortaköy

In Ortaköy

**

Photos from a trip to Trabzon, Rize and the Sumela Monastery:

View from the monastery

The Sumela Monastery

More views of the Monastery

Hills of çay (tea) plants in Rize

**

My boyfriend came to visit me around Christmas. We went to Cappadocia for part of his time in Turkey. This region is vastly different than the area that I live in. There is plenty of open landscape, and there was always a light layer of snow frosting the ground while we were there. The crazy pillars of phallic-shaped stones rise up all around the area. There are rock-cut chapels, and underground cities in this area as well.

These underground cities and chapels were settled at around 1800 B.C. to 1200 B.C., and these areas then became a refuge for Christians from the fourth to 11th centuries. The amount of history in that region is incredible.

Unfortunately, even a hot-air balloon ride over the rocky and snowy landscape couldn't lift my spirits. I was incredibly homesick; it was Christmas, and my first time away from my family during the holidays. My boyfriend and I weren't re-connecting in the way that I had hoped. When I think of Cappadocia now, I remember the cold, the feeling of isolation, my first earthquake tremor, and the smell of coal permeating the city of Göreme, where we stayed.

My boyfriend and I split up on New Year's Eve, and he decided to mention his plan to propose while we were in the hot air balloon in Cappadocia (because who doesn't love hearing that after a break up?). This was one of the prices that I had to pay for living this part of my life in Turkey.

Photos from Cappadocia:

View from the hotel

Walking to the Open Air Museum

2008.

In order to get away from the school for a little while, and to quench some thirst for travel, my co-worker Sarah and I went south to Antalya for a weekend. We rented a car, and navigated the jumbled streets of the city.

We stayed at a pension with a very hospitable owner. For our first breakfast he cooked eggs, put out tomatoes, cucumbers, olives, cheese, toast, and freshly-picked oranges (something the region is known for—it's fresh citruses).

Our first morning found us on our way to Termessos, an ancient city's ruins on the top of the Taurus mountains, with the Mediterranean glistening in the distance. I think these are the most beautiful ruins that I've seen.

We were the only two tourists there, and we had the whole site to ourselves. Our journey ended up being more of an exploratory hike, and the mountain air was invigorating. On our way out of the park, the security guards invited us in for çay. Since we were numb from the windy cold, we sat on the wooden floor of the tiny guard shack and enjoyed our tea before heading off to our next destination: the Karain Cave.

The Karain Cave was inhabited during the Paleolithic, Neolithic, and Bronze Age, as well as during Roman times. It's fascinating to think of humans living in this cave throughout so many ages...wondering how different the landscape looked then, what the people were like.

We stopped on the way to the cave to take photos of the mountains in the distance, only to end up attracting two men riding on a motorcycle. After we got back into the car, they slowed down, allowed us to pass them, and then proceeded to follow us. After Sarah sped up, we seemed to lose them. As we pulled into the parking lot at the cave (again, we were the only tourists), the motorcycle pulled up behind us. We paid our entrance fee, and hiked up to the cave, intent on ignoring the men (who were apparently friends with the man who sold us our tickets).

As we explored, our meditations on the cave were interrupted as we heard two other people approaching. It was the same two men. Up on top of a hill in a cave, alone, my mind began to plot ways to fight if the men attacked us. My hands were clasped around my keys in my pocket, the only thing that I could have used to protect myself. Sarah and I quietly marched out of the cave, as I made eye contact with one of the men and glared at him.

Walking down the hill, we were soon aware that they were again following us. We picked up the pace and bolted into our car, as they almost simultaneously got on their motorcycle. They continued to follow us, until Sarah picked up the speed in the car, and we finally lost them after merging onto the highway.

After the shaking and fuming subsided, we found ourselves back in Antalya, at a café with an orange grove near our pension. We sat and ate and drank wine to pass the rest of the afternoon. That evening, our pension owner made a feast for us, including fresh fish caught from the sea that day. We ate and drank and talked to another American traveler. It was lovely.

**

The following day, we drove the gorgeous route to Olympos, a quirky little town near the Mediterranean that is known for its tree house hotels and pensions. We explored another jungle-ridden compilation of ancient ruins and structures. We climbed up a cliff where we had superb views of the sea and the mountains behind us. I even learned to drive stick (uphill) on the way back to Antalya!

A beer and my first Turkish coffee at a beach-side café ended our trip to Antalya. Turkish coffee is essentially unfiltered espresso: there is a layer of mud-like grounds on the bottom of the cup when you finish drinking the coffee.

We drove to the airport and arrived back at our school that night.

Photos from Termessos:

On the drive up to Termessos

Ruins at Termessos

**

My first trip home that January was strange for me. It was the first time that I fully realized that I really had two separate lives. I had all of these people in Colorado who knew everything about me from childhood and through college, but no one there who knew who I was in Turkey. Then I had this whole set of people in Turkey, who knew me through working and living in the intimate environment of a boarding school, but knew nothing of my past. This was the first time that I realized how much can change when you leave home. My favorite bar in Fort Collins had closed. The bakery that I spent most of my college career working at had changed owners and was different. Nostalgia and loneliness were present in Colorado too, not just in Turkey.

**

The weather promptly changed once I returned from my holiday at home. February is a brutal month here. Our first weekend back, two co-workers got married, and I attended the reception in Istanbul. The night was spent drinking sangria and cosmopolitans, listening to live music in a small, classy, wooden-floored bar. When Sarah and I were ready to leave, two new acquaintances walked us back to our hotel in the foot of snow that had fallen that afternoon and evening. We trudged through the snow, occasionally slipping, and I was blissfully content—snow, in Turkey!

The next day, on the way back to school, it started to snow again. Five of us were packed into Tarragon and Sylvan's car (Tarra and Sylvan will become more important to my life story later), not feeling very pleasant after the previous evening's festivities, and more than a little grumpy.

The snow started to get worse and worse, until conditions were almost too dangerous to be driving in. As we pulled onto one of the bumpy dirt roads that led to the school, Sylvan decided that we couldn't drive any further, and pulled off the road. A driver from the school came and picked us up, and he took us the rest of the way to the school. There was at least a foot and a half of snow on the ground. It was the first time some of the students had ever seen snow.

**

Like I said, the weather changed after the break. All of a sudden, none of my co-workers were talking to me. Sarah, her friend Helga, and many of the other young teachers just ceased talking to me. Miscommunication and misunderstanding became drama and hurt feelings. All of a sudden, I was being shunned. I was 'flirting' with husbands and boyfriends, and more; I was breaking co-workers' hearts. Or so I was told. Funny how this all started happening when I became single. Almost simultaneously. When I was safely tucked away in a relationship, even if it was an overseas relationship, I was not a threat whatsoever.

At one point, I finally asked Sarah why everyone was blatantly avoiding me. She 'kindly' informed me that one woman was upset (this Helga character) because she thought I was flirting with her husband, and another co-worker thought that I flirted with **all** of the men on campus, no matter what the age range.

All of this came as a huge slap in the face to me. All of a sudden I was single, and all of a sudden I was Hester Pryne. Normally, it would be fine with me if people decided that I wasn't worth hanging out with. I was used to letting things like this bounce off and not stick. But when you're in the middle of nowhere, living and working with the same people, and don't have many other options for socialization, the shunning can be a problem.

This is when Tarra and Sylvan took me under their wings. They invited me to dinner one night, and asked me how I was doing. They made nachos, with cans of refried beans they had brought back from the States. I hadn't had nachos in what felt like years. Oh, how I'd missed tortilla chips and refried beans.

When I started telling Tarra how sorry I was if she ever thought I was flirting with Sylvan, she just laughed and told me that was absurd.

My colleague Helga liked to create drama, and had painted herself a fine masterpiece chock-full of it. One couple finally got over it (mostly), but the other three never did. And that was fine by me. Most of them broke their contracts and left after the first year was over anyway: Sarah, Helga, and her sidekick husband packed their things and were gone.

**

I thought that February was a tough month, but March was even harder. March is a series of days strung together that entail grey, drizzly, dismal forecasts. The sun is rarely out. I never felt so alone as I did my first March here.

I come home from class every day at around 4:00. There is nowhere to go in Gebze. There's only one bar, and it's for men. Going to Istanbul during the week is out of the question, it takes too long to get there and back. Even going to Istanbul on the weekends can be a drag. I usually go by myself, and that is just as isolating. How can you meet people in a foreign country where English is not the first language, and when my Turkish is minimal, despite my attempts to learn?

I found myself wallowing in a shallow, constant depression. I was haunted by memories of friends and family that I missed. I missed intimate friendships, and I missed being social. I missed companionship and being around people my own age. I had no idea how to fill my time. Cooking only took up so much space in the void, and I was still being shunned by most of my American colleagues.

**

Ghosts and haunts keep me awake at night. Phantom spiders crawl on my skin, and I bolt upright and toss sideways, and wipe them away from my body. As I lay me down to sleep, my mind's wheels start spinning and whirring out of control, and then, suddenly, sleep has escaped, and is flitting away, up toward the ceiling, leaving me down, down below. Wide-eyed and restless.

My breathing won't stabilize. My dreams won't come. I'd never had night terrors before, but I began to experience them now. Dogs breaking into my apartment and bumping up against my bed, snarling. I could feel my bed shaking in my dreams of half-sleep, half-reality. I was terrified to open my eyes to make the nightmares stop, just in case they were real.

Last night in my dream, my sister and I were in the back of a car being driven to my school, and she was in Turkey. It was so green and rural and beautiful. Then someone knocked on my door and I woke up. And my sister was no longer with me. She's still in Colorado and I'm still in Turkey, and she's joining the Air Force in August. And everything will change. And my little sister will be gone. And the last wisps of my childhood, our childhood, will be wrenched away.

**

My life resounds in clinking cups of tea, and the sounds of water spilling from a spout attached to a pot filled with hot, steaming leaves.

**

Being alone wasn't always overwhelming. Sometimes I would go to Istanbul and thrive off my solitude. I would watch the men selling fish while I waited for the ferry, walk from Taksim to Ortaköy, and buy a waffle, maybe drink coffee while perusing the sagging card tables holding up vast selections of used books. I could see a movie, or get a drink. These are also some of my dearest memories from my first year in Turkey. Being alone.

**

By the end of March I'd become so stressed about the situation with my co-workers, and so blue, that I started having sleep paralysis issues. I didn't realize that my nightmares bordering on vivid hallucinations were sleep paralysis. After a few nights of terrifying dreams, and avoiding sleep at all costs, I talked to Sylvan about it. He told me that it sounded like sleep paralysis. I looked up the symptoms, and that's what it was, sure enough. I couldn't sleep anymore at night because I was so worried about the nightmares that I would have. This was probably my lowest point that winter.

With what couldn't have been better timing, April arrived and I flew off to Tanzania to see my friend, Karen, who was in the Peace Corps in Tanzania at the time.

**

"A journey is a person in itself, no two are alike. And all plans, safe guards, policing, and coercion are fruitless. We find after years of struggle that we do not take a trip; a trip takes us...a trip, a safari, an exploration, is an entity, different from all other journeys. It has personality, temperament, individuality, uniqueness."

–*Travels with Charley in Search for America*, John Steinbeck.

I arrived in Dar Es Salaam on a Friday afternoon, and Karen and I went out for dinner at an Indian food restaurant. Seeing her was refreshing, revitalizing, and healing. We drank wine, and talked for a long time that night.

The following day we took a bus to Moshi (north, near Kenya). The views from the bus were phenomenal: lush green lands, beautiful gargantuan trees, women carrying baskets and loads of one thing or another on their heads. Everything moves even slower here than in Turkey, but without all of the pollution.

We drank warm ginger sodas through straws in glass bottles on the bus on our way to Moshi. We bought mangoes from a woman selling them on the road, and ate them while we walked.

We arranged a safari to go through Arusha and see Lake Manyara and Ngorongora crater on the following day.

**

The village outside of Lake Manyara was stunning to me. Karen and I took a walk before dinner one night. These adorable children said hi to us and then held our hands, one walked hugging my waist, and two followed us for about half of our stroll (apparently they wanted candy, but also our attention). There was such a sense of peace, the overwhelming beauty of dusk, the colorful Masaai in this village, Mto Wa Mbo (river of mosquitoes).

At dinner, we sat next to a man traveling who turned out to be from Turkey (but of course!). We ate our dinner with him, and afterward he prepared Turkish coffee for us. He was traveling with a canister of it...such a small world. It could fit into your palm.

I bought a kitange cloth that said in Swahili (roughly): "I won't worry about this now. I'll pick it up when I get time."

On our day at Lake Manyara, we saw stunning baobabs, storks, pelicans, zebras, Masaai giraffes, warthogs, impalas, hippos, bush elephants, vervet monkeys, blue collabus monkeys, plovers, grounded and grey hornbills, and a lioness in a tree, snoozing away the afternoon. Lake Manyara is the only place in the world where lions can be seen in trees.

Photos from Dar Es Salaam to Lake Manyara:

Baboons grooming

A blue monkey

Maasai giraffe

A dik dik

Dung beetle! Or as they call them in Tanzania...a 'shit-pusher'!

**

Perhaps the most striking part of our safari was the morning that we drove to Ngorangora Crater. We left early, and it was foggy and cloudy--not a good sign.

But, as we neared the park, it magically started to clear up, revealing the Serengeti to our left. It looked exactly as I had imagined it: vast, open plains, with an abundance of hidden creatures lurking in the tall yellow grasses. On our right was the crater. As we stood at the top and looked down into it, I was overcome with a deep feeling that I can't even describe. It looked like we had stepped into a photo or a film; surely this wasn't real.

As we descended into the park, it initially felt like an amusement ride to me, which was frustrating. I wanted it to feel natural.

We drove by some zebras and water buffalo, and they almost looked like they had been placed there for us. I had to keep reminding myself that they were real, that we were in the wild.

We saw hippos, cranes, and other beautiful birds. We rounded a corner and landed right in the middle of a family of lions. Not only adult males and females, but cubs too! Our guide said that we were incredibly lucky; he hadn't seen anything like it in years.

I finally got the pinch I needed to wake me out of my amusement park dream, when a full-grown male lion approached our vehicle. With our sunroof open and nothing to stop him from jumping onto the roof of our vehicle, I felt very humbled by his presence. Looking at the size of his paws made me shudder.

For our lunch, we sat outside, the winds whipping our skirts and hair around. A few hawks decided to start dive-bombing us for our lunch.

Ngorangora is one of the only places that I've ever felt absolutely breathless, completely overwhelmed by how stunning and perfect our planet is. The whole day, it felt as if time had stopped. The crater was almost other-worldly. I will cherish that day in my heart always.

Photos from Ngorangora:

A water buffalo and his egret friend

Hippo somersaulting in water.

Looking into the crater.

**

The rest of our trip consisted of shopping in markets, riding crowded buses to various destinations, and staying in a hut on the beach by the Indian Ocean for a night. That last night we ate dinner under the stars, and split a bottle of wine. The whole week had restored me, mentally and physically. Karen and I had satisfying conversations about all different subjects, and it was so good to spend time with someone outside of work. I came back to the school ready for the final couple of months of the school year.

**

Due to a series of unfortunate circumstances (or fortunate, depending on the perspective), I decided to buy my sister a ticket to Turkey. She stayed with me at the school for a couple of weeks, and we spent a long weekend on the Greek island of Chios.

Having my sister stay with me did wonders for my mental health. She came to some of my classes, met my students, and hung out with me at night. I had a four-day weekend while she was here, and we took the opportunity to travel to the Aegean region of Turkey, where we caught a ferry to Chios, a Greek island off the coast of Turkey. We spent the few days we had driving a rental around the island (well, she drove, since it was manual, and she was semi-successful in that endeavor), going to beaches where the water was freezing cold and we absolutely did not catch a tan, and going out to the plethora of restaurants with an abundance of Greek men at night.

Having my sister here was a wind of warm changes. Making coffee in my miniature French press for two people instead of one in the morning was comforting. Knowing that she was sleeping in the room next to me while I was getting ready for class provided such solace. I was no longer alone.

Students came over and taught us how to make gözleme; other students came over and made us Turkish coffee (and read our fortunes for us. Mine, a dolphin, predicted a boyfriend in my future...that was two years ago, and I'm still waiting).

I have such fond memories of Chios and Çesme with Gener, the hospitable Turk who worked at the ferry station, offering us green plums, driving us to and picking us up from the ferry station; Leonidas, my sister's bartender friend who proved to be dangerously generous in his line of work; hearing OneRepublic blaring into the night sky while we were out and walking around.

**

My sister left a couple of nights ago. We had a lovely last evening together in Istanbul prior to her departure.

It was a sunshine-y, warm day, the Bosphorus was beautiful, and the air was clear. We explored the hustle and bustle of the Egyptian Spice Bazaar (I much prefer this bazaar to the insanity of the Grand Bazaar). While gazing at the assorted plants (tomatoes, basil, and parsley--oh my!), we couldn't help but notice the giant jars of ...leeches?, hanging out by the plants and gardening supplies.

The inside of the bazaar is adorned with Turkish delight, spices galore (cumin, peppers, curry, mint, and oodles more), honeycomb, teas, and random gift items (bowls, pashminas) for purchasing or perusing.

On her last night, we had dinner by the Bosphorus on a lovely, clear evening.

At one point, our waiter came up to us while we were eating, and pointed excitedly out to the water. A handful of dolphins were swimming in a cluster past the restaurant. Maybe the students had misinterpreted my fortune. Maybe there were real dolphins in my future.

She left the next morning, and I was by myself once more.

**

Forgive this segment, as I'm on a temporary downward coast on this part of my journey's constant roller coaster cycle.

Traveling around with my sister brought to light a whole new experience...not necessarily because she has blond hair and blue eyes, but because, as I was told by a co-worker, two women are more approachable than just one. I had become so used to my traveling solo invisibility, that I had forgotten how to deal with being approached.

And, my, have we been approached.

And gawked at. Leered at.

I'm a little burnt out on being a foreign, young female at this point. There's only so many prodding Turkish men that I want to politely converse with until I can nicely say goodbye. It's gotten to the point where I've started saying "git" (go away) and don't even feel bad about it. But really, you'd think they'd take the hint from my angry glares and blatant non-interest.

It's starting to warm up in Turkey; it's been in the 80's this week. Riding on the train for an hour with groceries (fretting about their state of non-refrigeration) can make someone slightly cranky. That someone being me. So can the potent aroma of b.o. and wailing children on the slightly claustrophobic, motion-sickness-inducing train.

So can coming home to an apartment where every time I open the refrigerator, the freezer cover falls on my toes, where there are little flies and bugs crawling or flying in each room, where my toilet has ceased to work (or flush), and so, being in a place where actual plungers don't exist can be slightly irritating.

Credit card machines are not accepting my foreign cards, ATM's are sometimes not able to dispense cash, I'm not able to just drive to the grocery store in my own car with air conditioning, there are men constantly muttering Turkish at me under their breath...these things can also make a person cranky.

I've realized that I am in a cultural limbo. I don't have enough of a grasp on the Turkish language to come anywhere near not being an outsider, and even if I did, I would still be a 'yabancı' (foreigner).

But now, due to a measly, recent conversation with two American boys this weekend, I realized that I've also alienated myself from my own culture. With some of their brilliant comments such as: "It's like we're in a foreign country," while sitting at a restaurant in *Turkey*, it struck me that, maybe it's getting harder for me to relate to Americans, period. There is a chance that it was just those particular ones, the ones who only have these brilliant comments to utter.

Or, how about the American in the Greek army that my sister and I met on Chios, who (when the election came up) proceeded to talk about how women shouldn't run for the presidency because of their PMS-ing "disability..."?

Where does this leave me?

I am becoming a cultural mutt, without a constant or stable identity.

**

Throughout my first year, I often thought about getting a pet. Tarra and Sylvan had a cat, and that seemed like a great idea. Cats are low-maintenance, easy to transport, and are good company. The thought of having another living, breathing being in my home was very appealing.

A student of mine gave me a male kitten from a litter that her family's cat had in May. He was absolutely adorable. When I originally saw him, I thought that he was a girl, so I wanted to name him Lale (la-lay), which means tulip. After a few days passed, and I realized he was a boy, I gave him the name Can (John), which means life or love or soul. Technically, his name was Lale Can.

Having an animal around does enigmatically wonderful things for the mind and spirit. I swear I could feel my stress level going down; I could sense the anxiety evaporating from my body. I only had time to spend a month with Can before it was summer vacation, where I would go to the U.S. for a couple of months, but the month that I had with him was beautiful. He spent the summer with a co-worker (Serkan, actually).

And so, my companion was found.

**

Cuma pazarı: The Friday market in Gebze. For almost every week of my stay here, this market has made me incredibly happy and appreciative.

Tarra and I started going to the market in May. We usually go every other Friday (on average). Even when she can't go, I go alone, because it's probably the only thing that I really enjoy about Gebze.

Yards and yards of fresh produce line a street that goes on forever. Fresh apples, bananas, grapefruit, lemons, oranges, tomatoes, squash, broccoli, spinach, eggplant, potatoes, onions, fresh garlic, cheeses, eggs, fish, spices, nuts....the colorful array of delicious edibles goes on and on.

It's wonderful, because I can gauge where we are in terms of seasons (and, in turn, the school year), because everything sold here is seasonal. In the fall, there are giant squash that resemble pumpkins, and I can make pumpkin muffins, pumpkin cookies, and pumpkin bread with fresh supplies. Come late

March, the artichokes start to appear, so steamed artichokes with garlic bread become a staple meal for me. April brings the strawberries, and I eat strawberry shortcake with coffee for breakfast every weekend until they're gone. May brings the cherries that I'd never liked before, but love now. It's something to look forward to every week: stocking up on fresh produce that I will use in my meals until the next Friday market. The excellent part about going on Friday is that I started making pizza every Friday night (a tradition that I borrowed, or stole, from Tarra and Sylvan), and I use the fresh cheese and produce that I just purchased hours before. Eating seasonally, and eating fresh, local produce is something that I will miss when I leave.

**

Completely homesick by June, all I wanted was to leave Turkey. After the seniors graduated and the other students left, the campus was quiet, desolate and lonely. I had IB training in Athens in early July, but had some time to kill beforehand, so I decided to go to Prague. I had heard wonderful things about Prague, and it was a place that I'd always wanted to see.

For a few days, I headed north to see the Czech Republic.

Unfortunately, my impression of the city was that, despite its beautiful architecture and landscapes, it was cold and unfriendly. I've never felt so alone. I even missed the comfort of feeling alone in my own apartment in Turkey. I tried to enjoy the food (bagels and Mexican food is what I sought, after months of being deprived of these two favorite things while living in Turkey), but neither the food nor the Charles Bridge made me feel better.

All I really remember of Prague is beautiful classical music, churches, and coldness.

**

"Our correspondences show us where our intimacies lie. There is something very sensual about a letter. The physical contact of

pen to paper, the time set aside to focus thoughts, the folding of
the paper into an envelope, licking it closed, addressing it, a
chosen stamp, and then the release of the letter to the mailbox
are all acts of tenderness.
And it doesn't stop there. Our correspondences have wings-
paper birds that fly from my house to yours-flocks of ideas
crisscrossing the country. Once opened, a connection is made.
We are not alone in the world."
-- *Refuge*, by Terry Tempest Williams

**

This mystery only seems to
grow
more complex
and futile
as time snowballs by,
laughing at that
wadded up
newspaper,
lying in the gutter,
sewage seeping
onto the creased
pages,
smeared
over
the well-articulated
words.

Alone in a city that
creaks,
cobblestone roads
beneath my
weary, aching
please rest
bones.

My joints are

sighing
My body-
confusion-
Where?
Why am I
even
in this
place.
Is this
some test?

The temptations
and struggles,
but no way to
even attain those
lusty
wanderings.

Instead, the
delicious bait
dangles in front
of me,
but I can't
reach it,
it's too...
foreign.
so sickeningly out of reach.

I don't belong here
and it shows.
I don't belong any
where
any
more.

So I sip this wine
to enter a
hazy phase

Where I don't
hear
the accordion's
melancholy
pumping
back
and forth-

Where I no longer see
the couples
swaying
to
and
fro.

Or at least I trick myself into believing I don't.

My almost-empty
glass
gazes back at me.
The only
companion
that I have in
this moment
is a glass
and a book
and my pen.

And three crimson droplets.

Where did this
deep
unearthly desire
come from?
That fated me
to
do

this
alone.

I am a laughable site
to see.

The loneliest sounds
in a city
are the trams,
tunneling by on
those lone silver tracks

An ambulance
wailing,
singing
out
to the clock
towers,
looming
above.

Footsteps
pattering
on the
path
to an empty
hotel room.

But,
sometimes,
the bow
glides
effortlessly
over the
strings.

And the wind...

it just
tingles.

**

(Sunrise leaving Fort Collins, CO)

After 39 days of being home (well, minus the 10 days spent in Costa Rica with my parents), I am headed back to the land of baklava and çay.

I have mixed emotions about returning. Part of me is excited: excited to see the students again, excited to see friendly co-workers, to go on my runs around the school, to see my little cat, to cook in my kitchen again, to be challenged by the new classes I'll be teaching this year, and I'm excited to be going to a semi-familiar place this time, instead of going in cold.

On the other hand, the days that I spent at home were beautiful. I stared at the beautiful Colorado skies as long as possible, I was able to smell rain and freshly-mowed grass. I was able to re-connect with new and old friends, which was both re-affirming and encouraging. I was able to see my beautiful Colorado mountains again, and breathe in the clean, mile-high air. I rode my bike around Ft. Collins, and visited old favorite spots.

But, I know that I'm ready to go back. It's time to start a new year, face new challenges, and experience new stories to tell.

Thanks & Acknowledgments:

Thank you to Serkan, Tarra, and Sylvan, for being the best support system someone could ask for in the middle of nowhere, and in a foreign country. I miss being within a close proximity to you on a regular basis!

Thank you to J, my high school English teacher and newspaper advisor, who told me about her experiences teaching overseas, and planted this seed when I was just 16.

Thank you to my gin martini gal, BG, who so thoughtfully perused this piece of writing before I felt semi-secure enough to publish it.

Made in the USA
Middletown, DE
30 September 2023

39840393R00069